BLUEPRINT
TO
SUCCESS

How a 16-year old Prepared, Learned, and Started a Business in 21 Days

Mason James Butler

AUTHOR OF
*The Insider's Guide to
Editing the Perfect Podcast*

DEDICATION:
To
Dr. Paul Barlow
Thanks for believing in me
(And for giving me an A)

This publication is designed to provide accurate and authoritative information in regard to the subject matter covered. It is sold with the understanding that the publisher is not engaged in rendering legal, accounting, or other professional service. If legal advice or other expert assistance is required, the services of a professional should be sought.

Butler, Mason James
Blueprint to Success: How a 16-Year Old Prepared, Learned, and Started a Business in 21 Days
ISBN: 978-1507715628
    1.   Business
    2.   Entrepreneurship

INTRODUCTION

This is a book filled with principles that I have learned from great men and leaders, how I've learned a new skill and have begun to make money from it, and how I've launched a business in three weeks. It details each lesson I've found critical in the seven books that I read, some of my story, and how you too can start now to get the results that you want in any area of your life, whether it be business related, personal, or financial.

Let me first share with you what I learned over the summer of 2014. I learned the power of goal setting, because of my great desire and ambition to get a new computer. I spent countless hours poring over every website I could find about computers, soaking in information about every part and system. I saw what looked cool to me, and I wanted to work for it. I could already mow a lawn well for my parents, so why couldn't I do it for someone else? With this in my mind, I set out and began to work on getting clients, but I'll talk about that a little later.

After one summer, I made almost $1,200. That may not seem like a lot, but at that time of my life, it was the most money I had ever made, all within the frame of a few short months. I beamed with happiness as my parts arrived, and it was even more fun as I put it together over six hours. It was beautiful, and it was mine.

One of the reasons I decided to start my second business, Mason James Media, was to have a business that I could work on year round, and not just have seasonal work. I could also use my new computer to help me in the building of my business, and to generate income from the talents I have with computers.

When I first proposed my independent study project to my Vice-Principal Mr. Simmons, he seemed skeptical. But, I knew that any goal was within my reach, as long as I work hard at it, with smart goals built around it. I've set the goal of making $1000 a month and after the first three weeks, I have already earned my first $200.

In this book, I will go over in detail of what I learned from these books, how I learned to edit podcasts, and how I launched my business from the startup phase. This book is to show that anyone can have success, no matter how old, young, or whatever level you feel you can play at. You can start now.

In Part I, I'll share the seven books I read and the lessons I learned from each one. In Part II, I'll share about how I learned the skill of podcasting. In Part III, I'll share my business plan. In Part IV, I'll share documents I used to set up my business and get started.

The book will detail what I learned over the course of these three weeks and how I put my business together in 21 days. *This book is literally the bomb diggety.* I hope you enjoy it!

Blueprint to Success
How a 16-Year Old Prepared, Learned and Started a Business in 21 Days

The first thing I did as to prepare to start my new business was to read several business books which my dad recommended. Here is a brief synopsis of what I learned from each one:

Book 1:
The Slight Edge by Jeff Olson

The Slight Edge is a half self-help book, other half business book. It teaches about principles that Jeff Olson has learned and applied throughout his life, and that they all seemed to point to one universal law that he always missed; the big difference between the very poor and the very rich (Hint, hint, it's not money).

Most notably, and like almost all entrepreneurs, Jeff started from nothing. When he was a young adult, he dropped out of college. If you knew him at the time, you could probably tell that he didn't have much of a future. He didn't apply himself anywhere. After he dropped out of college, he moved to Miami, the Spring Break capital of the world. To become, of all things, a beach bum. At the time, he was someone who chased girls and lifted weights, hanging out on the beach all day. He called himself "Gorgeous George," after a Wrestling champion that brought the sport to TV. George (The Bum) got a job cutting grass at the Orland Country Club to support himself.

One day, while he was working hard under the burning sun, he noticed something odd. He stopped doing his work for a moment, and observed the people playing golf. He saw the upper class driving over his freshly cut grass in golf carts.
As he saw them playing and laughing on the golf course, a question began to well up inside of him:

"Why?" He thought. "Why is it that they're over there riding in carts, and I'm over here working? I don't get it!"

What had they done so they could have fun, while he was working? Were they just better than him? Did they work twenty times as hard? Were they twenty times smarter? Probably not. But then there had to be a difference!

Then it clicked. He saw a small piece of a much larger puzzle. Not enough to finish it, but enough to get started on the road to success. He realized the big difference between why he was so flat out broke, and why they were living in comfort. He decided right then that he was never going back to the way he was.

Up until this point in his life, he thought that he was pretty mediocre. He had average grades, average athletic ability, and average social skills. He knew that if he ever wanted to become anybody, he would have to work harder and be more persistent than anyone he knew.

With this in mind, he set out to accomplish his dreams. He went straight back to college, and he worked harder than ever to make his dreams a reality. He had graduated at the top of his school in business class, and went on to work at an international airport, working hard, until he became one of the youngest international airport managers in the country. He was such hot stuff, that Texas Instruments, a giant corporation situated in Dallas, later recruited him. By now, he felt that he was pretty much unstoppable, so he started his own solar company in New Mexico. Although he knew nothing about solar energy, how hard could it be?

Apparently, not much. Through his principles of hard work and discipline, in two years his company went on to be one of the largest solar energy companies in America.

And he lived happily ever after... And the rest is history. Or is it?

No, it wasn't the end. Things changed for him. Tax laws shifted, times changed. Before he knew it, the company that he had built from zero to millions seemed gone overnight. He was deep in debt.

He was even more broke than when he was the Beach Bum!
He felt angry. Pieces of his life lay shattered on the ground, and he knew that he had to make sense of it. What made the difference? Why wasn't he still successful? What was it that he did wrong?

Hmm....

Why was it that he could be both the Beach Bum, and the Millionaire? What was the difference between those two men, Even though they each were the same guy?

This wasn't a total Epiphany for him. It wasn't an immediate call to action, or a quick fix like last time. This time was methodical and well thought out.

In fact, the answer was so simple that most people miss it. In fact, 95% of people miss it. About One in Twenty people report actually being happy with the life they have. *Only one.* How could this be? Then he discovered why so many people have been falling in and out of success, seeming so inconsistently.

It was their habit. That's all it ever was. When he realized that he needed that change, he worked hard, and used proper habits to get where he wanted to go. Then, he stopped doing them. When you stop making that daily progress in the right direction, your life is going in the down direction. It's simple. You either go up or down. There is no middle. The habits that got him to survive could have been the habits that made him thrive, if only he kept doing them.

When people get so sick of where there life is at a current point, they can only go up. It's the only option. So they do whatever it takes to get out of the pit. They climb viscously out of the hole that they dug.

They create habits to stop themselves from becoming like that again. Then, when they are at the top of the world, living their dreams and goals, they fall back down again.

Why?
They got comfortable. They started to choose the easier things, instead of the things that made them better. They started getting lazy, and not working as hard to keep up that level up success.

Recently, the New Year just started. Millions of Americans will be making resolutions, and quitting after the first few weeks. Why is that? Because they don't understand why habits matter.

They are too busy looking for the magic "Cure all," the "Magic Bullet", or the "Quantum leap." They are too busy looking for the cure all to notice the little small things that often make the biggest difference. Too often, people look for the one step shortcut to get what they want. We live in a world that holds too dear to them the philosophy that they can just 'Push the button', and get instant gratification.

This is why many fall short. When people attempt to get things done, they seek the easier option. They fall short. Successful people know that any success has to be worked hard for, and will not just fall into their lap.

This is part of his next point, is that point of success is easy, and failure is easy. Every single choice we make, day by day, brings us closer to an end that can be hard to see.

Success is really not hard to get to. And at the same time, hard too. It's surprisingly easy to go for a fifteen-minute job, but it's also easy to flick on the TV.

This is what Jeff Olson calls the slight edge. The ideology is simple, as is most of the things found in his book. In fact, most of the principles are so stupidly simple, its ridiculous. And that's why most people miss it.

Success is not really a nebulous thing. Most people think that "Someday" is the only option for them. 'When I have enough money, I'll... When I have enough talent, I'll...'

If "Someday" is not another "Today," then it will never happen. You already have the knowledge, skill, and talent to start now. You already know what step one is. You already know everything that you should do <u>now,</u> to be able to get the success you desire. He states this many times, and uses this quote by Ralph Waldo Emerson to back him up- "Do the thing, and you shall have the power."

Or, even the company Nike's slogan: "Just do it."

The real difference between successful people and unsuccessful people is that successful people do what unsuccessful people are not willing to do. We live in a society of instant gratification, where it is much easier to eat the donut, and sleep in, than to eat the salad, and wake up early.

Successful people know about the slight edge. They don't use those exact words, but they know the guiding principles: What you do daily matters. Unsuccessful people hope it doesn't matter.

Setting habits that create success are boring at first. In fact, so boring that you can't see a difference at first. Although we can't see it in the moment, over time, and with continual effort, is how great things come to be.

Think about the smallest stream, or something to that effect. Think about how little and insignificant it seems to anyone who sees it. It may not look like much then. Now think about the Grand Canyon (I've heard that postcards don't do it justice, that you really have to see it to believe it). The only difference between these two forces of nature is *time. The only difference between a small stream and a gigantic canyon is time.*

Many people mistake time as their enemy. That time is always working against them. That's not entirely true. The reason that time is not in their side is because the slight edge is working against them. Small mistakes in judgment, compounded over time, will become an unstoppable force. We all know that smoking will kill us, or that eating too many cheeseburgers can kill us too.

The main problem is that it doesn't kill us right then, right now.

Unsuccessful people do not see the value in the time that they have. They do not see why those little choices matter, until the giant compounded effect is sitting right on their door. Successful people know that 'If it's going to be, then it's up to me.' And they put in those daily steps to reach their goals.

The slight edge gives back over time what you put into it.

Many people in our culture think that success is based upon luck. Successful people know that they are responsible for the outcome in their lives. All what some people call "Luck", is really just doing small actions daily: compounded over time. It is that constancy of being prepared from those small disciplines that will eventually create opportunity.

Our culture worships "The Big Break." Unsuccessful people do not realize the value of cultivating something, and being patient on waiting for the results. Anything that looks like a breakthrough is the result of hundreds of little steps. No success is immediate or instantaneous; no collapse is sudden or precipitous. Everything you do is a product of the slight edge.

Your thoughts determine your actions. 99.9% of all of our actions are turned over to our subconscious habits. Our habits define who we are. If you aren't aware of them, they are most likely bad ones.

First, it starts out by which thoughts you allow to have in your mind. If you choose to think negative thoughts, then you will have a negative life. If you have positive thoughts, you will find more opportunity, and better results. It is the law of cause and effect. Nothing is truly out to "get you." What you put in is what you get out. Once you have set a certain standard for thinking, your thoughts become your actions. Your actions become your habits; your habits become your life choices, which ultimately become your life.

Fortunately, our conscious brain can reprogram subconscious actions. This is sometimes referred to as "going out of our comfort zone." The thing with humans is that they will try desperately to stay in their comfort zones, no matter what.

When I started my lawn mowing business, one of my friends wanted to be partners with me. However, he didn't really want to go out and do the work. So, I decided not to be partners with him. He wasn't going to contribute and wasn't willing to get out of his comfort zone. I designed and printed off over 400 flyers and spent six hours under the burning sun going door-to-door delivering flyers. It was painful, and although I got blisters and got sunburned, it paid off. I remember how surprised and excited I felt when I got my first client. Over time, and with 800 more flyers delivered, I got new clients and I started making more money. Eventually I was able to pay cash for my new computer, which I had been planning on buying. It was an exciting moment.

The point of that story is that when you take action, you are rewarded. Sure, it may be a little harder to do those good disciplines, but it's much easier in the long run on you. It will seem hard to discipline yourself to get out there and get the work done, but ultimately, it will be worth it. It is better to move and make mistakes than to stay standing still. You can start living your goals and dreams now. This book teaches that principle profoundly; Start now. Get good results later.

Anyone can find that change they desire. Try to examine all areas of your life. Your relationships, career, hobbies, happiness, and any success in any area of life attributes, you will find the slight edge at work. Whether it is working for or against you is completely up to you. Many will refute this. Those people who won't have success in their lives will blame everybody and everything but themselves.

It may sometimes be easier to see that in others than in us. This is a way of thinking that can be changed, just like the rest of our habits. Each of us wants to be that strong person we envision, and the only thing that is truly keeping us down, day after day, is ourselves. Theodore Roosevelt said:

"If you could kick the person in the pants responsible for most of your trouble, you wouldn't sit for a month."

This quote made me laugh. I thought about all the things in my life that I would definitely kick if I had the chance. Then I realized it was all up to me, and that changed a lot of my thinking.

All in all, this book teaches about the principles needed for success in any area of your life. It does not claim to be some "magic get ahead quick guide (because there are enough of those)". This is just a law of the Universe. I would recommend this book to anyone who wants to live their dreams, who want to be better in any aspect of their life, who want more out of life, anyone who wants to be rich, anyone who wants to be happy, and whoever wants a little more out of life. This book is such a wonderfully written masterpiece about how the slight edge can help you get whatever you want out of life, no matter who you are. As long as you stick to it, and as you are always continuously improving.

So- in the end, what is the difference between the beach bum, and the millionaire inside each of us? It is our daily actions, compounded over time.

"I didn't change who I was, as much as I changed what I did.

Book 2:
How I Raised Myself From Failure to Success in Selling
By Frank Bettger

How I Raised Myself From Failure To Success In Selling is a classic read on selling that I would recommend to anyone who wants to be successful in their career, in their friend and family relationships, and anyone who's interested in debate. In fact, if you've ever heard of *How to Win Friends and Influence People*, that author, Dale Carnegie, was good friends with Bettger, and encouraged him to write this book. Although it was written in 1949, its principles still stand true to this day.

Bettger was one of the most successful life insurance salespeople of his time. His father died when he was young, so he helped his his mother pay the bills for himself, and four siblings. He had no formal education after the sixth grade, but eventually found his way into selling. His initial efforts to sell insurance were a dismal failure, until he learned the secrets that helped him turn his career around into becoming successful.

Here are five critical lessons about selling I learned from this book:

1) **Convey enthusiasm in everything you do. Enthusiasm is the key to sales.**

Frank Bettger's story at the beginning of the book about the power of enthusiasm is one of my favorite parts of the book. He was fired from a professional baseball team and he had the courage to go and ask his manager why. His manager told him that he was fired because he was lazy! This answer shocked Bettger because this was the last thing he thought he would ever hear him say. Bettger admitted the reason he didn't play with enthusiasm was because he was nervous, and was trying to hide his fear from the crowd.

His manager told him that hiding his nervousness would never work and that if he ever wanted to be successful that he needed to "put some life and enthusiasm into his work!"

He got a job in the minor leagues with a pay cut that was seven times less than what he had been making. He decided to take his old manager's advice and he started acting enthusiastic.

It is said that when he took the field, he acted "like a man electrified." He acted as though he was "alive with a million batteries." He played so well that 10 days after acting with tremendous amounts of enthusiasm, his income increased 700% and he got the nickname of "Pep" Bettger.

A couple of years later, he played 3rd base for the St. Louis Cardinals and had increased his income by more than thirty times. He asks, "What did it? Enthusiasm alone did it; nothing but enthusiasm." -- *How I Raised Myself from Failure to Success in Selling*, p. 11.

He said three things happened as a result of his acting enthusiastically:

1) My enthusiasm almost entirely overcame my fear. In fact my nervousness began to work for me and I played far better than I ever thought I was capable of playing. (If you are nervous, be thankful. Don't hold it back. Turn it on. Let your nerves work for you).

2) My enthusiasm on the team affected the other players on the team, and they too became enthusiastic.

3) ...I felt better during the game and after it was over than I had ever felt before." --*How I Raised Myself from Failure to Success in Selling*, p. 10.

He talks about how amazed he was in the beginning about how he didn't get more talented at first; he just put forth the energy that was lacking, and his true ability came out later.

Two years after that, he broke his arm and he was forced to give up baseball. He eventually began selling life insurance (which he later stated that that was one of the best things to ever happened to him). His first ten months were "the longest and most disheartening months of my life." He thought of quitting and figured that he "was never cut out to be a salesman", and started to think about finding another line of work.

Before doing so, he decided one night to go to a Dale Carnegie course in public speaking. That night changed his life because Mr. Carnegie told him to talk with more enthusiasm. This experience reminded him of his time playing baseball and his fault of going through the motions without enthusiasm. He reflected that this was threatening to wreck his career in selling just like it did in baseball. He made the decision that night to put the same amount of enthusiasm into selling insurance that he did when he got demoted to the minor leagues.

He determined his next prospect would meet the most enthusiastic salesman of his entire life. As a result, the man bought. Listen to what Bettger says:

"From that day on, I began to sell. The Magic of Enthusiasm began to work for me in business, just as it had in Baseball."

He continues: "When I force myself to act enthusiastic, I soon feel enthusiastic. During my thirty-two years of selling, I have seen enthusiasm double and triple the income of dozens of salesmen, and I have seen the lack of it cause hundreds of salesmen to fail. **I firmly believe enthusiasm is by far the biggest single factor in successful selling.**"--*How I Raised Myself from Failure to Success in Selling*, p. 13.

This part of the book helped me realize that I needed to act more enthusiastically about things in my life if I wanted to see a dramatic change, and that if I acted more enthusiastically, than others around me would act accordingly. The result for me will be nothing less than increased sales, better friendships, and more positivity in my life that will make me even more excited and enthusiastic as I reach my goals.

This book taught me that enthusiasm, and showing how happy you are is one of the biggest factors in successful selling.

2) Selling narrows down to seeing new prospects that can buy what I sell.

When Frank was in a sales slump, he felt ready to quit again. The one thing that changed and made a massive difference was that he went to one last company meeting. Then, Walter LeMar Talbot, President of the Insurance Company, spoke at the meeting, changing Frank's life forever. "Gentlemen, after all, this business of selling narrows down to one thing - just one thing . . . seeing the people! Show me any man of ordinary ability who will go out and earnestly tell his story to four or five people every day, and I will show you a man who just can't help making good!"

Frank discovered that seeing four or five people a day was a big job. In order to keep on track, he found it was critically important for him to keep good records. By tracking the results of his calls, he was able to improve his closing ratio from one sale out of 29 calls to one out of three. He increased his closing ratio by 10 times, because he applied some of the slight edge principles.

This book helped me learn that everything that I will do in sales, is largely determined that I see the right people, and see them as often as I can. Over the course of my Independent Study, I realized that it isn't enough to have a great product. You have to get the message out there to relevant people to get the number of sales you need.

3) Find out what the person wants and then help them find the best way to get it.

There is a great statement made in the book: "When you show a man [or woman] what he [or she] wants, he'll [or she'll] move heaven and earth to get it."-- *How I Raised Myself from Failure to Success in Selling*, p. 43.

On one of his sales calls, Frank hit a "home run." He made one of the largest sales in the history of his company to that point, reaching his financial goal in one sale what he wanted to make in *one year*. In analyzing the sale, he wasn't able to determine what had happened, or why he sold so well. Later on, when he went to a conference to talk about the great sales success he had, an older fellow by the name of Clayt Hunsicker, pointed out to Frank the reason for the sale. This completely changed his understanding about selling, and my understanding of human relations. Clayt said, "The most important secret of salesmanship is to find out what the other fellow wants, then help him find the best way to get it . . . If you will always remember this one rule, selling will be easy."

This taught me that the best way to get what I want out of selling is by being a good listener, a friend to my potential client, and finding out what they really want, by listening, and by being patient. I talk about it a little bit better in the next section here:

4) **Overcome objections by asking questions.**

I liked this statement that Bettger made on pages 45 and 46 of the book, when referring to an excellent salesperson named Elliott Hall who gave a demonstration of how he met objections:

"He met these objections by asking questions. He didn't attempt to tell his objectors that they were wrong and show them how much smarter he was than they. He simply asked questions with which his objectors had to agree. And he kept on asking questions until the answers added up to just one conclusion—a sound conclusion based on facts.

"The profound lesson I learned from that master salesman changed my whole way of thinking. He never gave the impression that he was trying to persuade or influence anybody to his way of thinking. Elliott Hall's questions had only one purpose: 'To help the other fellow recognize what he wants, then help him decide how to get it.'" *--How I Raised Myself from Failure to Success in Selling*, pp. 45-46.

Here are six things Bettger says you can gain by the question method:

1. Questions help you avoid arguments.
2. Questions help you avoid talking too much.
3. Questions enable you to help the prospect recognize what he wants. Then you can help him decide how to get it.
4. Questions help crystallize the prospect's thinking. The idea becomes his idea.
5. Questions help you find the most vulnerable point with which to close the sale—the key issue.
6. Questions give the prospect a feeling of importance. When you show him that you respect his opinion, he is more likely to respect yours."*--How I Raised Myself from Failure to Success in Selling*, p. 62.

This is one of the great "legendary secrets" to becoming a debater, or being a lawyer, or being a good friend. You need to ask the probing questions that will evoke the answers that you need.

5) Have a system for personal development and make it a part of your daily routine.

Frank concludes the book by revealing a key secret of his success. As a resident of Philadelphia, he was fascinated with one of Philadelphia's most famous historical figures, Benjamin Franklin. Franklin only had two years of formal education and became one of the leading scholars and statesmen of his time.

When reading *The Autobiography of Benjamin Franklin,* Bettger noticed that Benjamin Franklin wrote about a system he used for his personal development. Franklin dedicated more space relating to this idea - fifteen pages - than anything else in the book, said he owed all of his success and happiness to the system, and concluded, "I hope, therefore, that some of my descendants may follow the example and reap the benefit." Franklin described a system where he chose thirteen subjects and focused on improving on each one for a week at a time, leaving the rest to chance, or his current habit. At the end of thirteen weeks, he would repeat the procedure, completing four "sets" in a year.

It's fascinating to me to see this goes back to the principles taught in the slight edge, that having a planned, time oriented discipline system for yourself will help you to achieve the goals that you set. It's fascinating to me to see all of these great men finding solutions to their problems by identifying the need, writing down the steps they need to take over a set period of time, and taking the steps one at a time.

I hope that I can apply some of the fantastic principles found in this book, and that as I start my new business, and build better relationships, that I can always show that enthusiasm to those I listen to, and to serve those that I sell to.

Book 3:
Advanced Selling Strategies by Brian Tracy

Brian Tracy's *Advanced Selling Strategies* is a book on how to better improve your overall salesmanship. He talks a lot about the best ideas he has found over his life to increase your sales, and to make your time more effective.

You can learn anything you need to learn to achieve any goal by finding out what others have done before you to get the results you want to get. This is the first rule that he talks about, coined by Socrates as the Law of Causality. We know it better as the Law of Cause and Effect.

The key to success is to learn from the experts. I learned that you should study and copy the very best people in your field. Do what they do, day after day until it becomes second nature, and you will begin to get the same results.

A lot of what success boils down to is how and where you spend your time. Successful people know that getting where you want to go will take less time if you focus 20% of your effort on the 80% that will give you the best results. This is often called the Pareto principle.

Brian Tracy states that "Fully 80% of your success as a salesperson will be determined by attitude, and 20% by your aptitude. A positive mental attitude, or a constructive and optimistic way of looking at yourself and your work, goes hand in hand with sales success in any field."-*Advanced Selling Strategies*, p. 27.

The quality of your thinking will affect and determine the quality of the life you live. Henry Ford states this well:

'Whether you think you can, or you think you can't--you're right.'

Successful people are aware that wherever they want to be in life, can be achieved, if they break it down into daily, doable steps. You have (whether you are aware of it or not), miniature self-concepts that you think about how high you can perform in every area of your life. Your behavior will always conform in a manner consistent to the way that you see yourself. This is what Brian Tracy refers to as a "Mental Makeup."

This "Mental Makeup" consists of your self-ideal, self image, and self esteem.

The self-ideal is a conglomeration of every single ideal that you think a 'great' person could belong to. Your subconscious is working all the time to become this person, whether you like it or not. Studies show that you will become just like the five people you associate with the most with on average. Successful people know this, and will stay away from people who are toxic to their success. These are those who are petty in their thinking, and who mock those that aspire to success. This will ultimately drag them down.

The next, is your self-image. This is what he refers to as "your inner mirror." You will behave on the outside in a manner consistent with the picture that you have on the inside. The moment that you change the thinking of having a roof on what you can and can't achieve is the moment that you will achieve sales success.

The third is your self-esteem. This is the energy source of your inner power, the key to success in life. This is defined as how much you like yourself. I discovered from reading this book that if who you want to be and what you are doing is consistent, then you will like and respect yourself. Selling is all in the mind and how you present yourself.

I learned that ultimately you control who you are through your thoughts. What you allow to go in your mind is what will become real through your actions.

Next, I learned about how consultants view themselves versus how salespeople view themselves. Successful salespeople know that they are consultants. Consultants are experts and authorities in their fields. They invest time to learn their products inside and out. They spend time learning what their competition sells versus what they sell. They know the features, benefits, strengths, and shortcomings of what they offer. Top salespeople are resources for their clients. They see themselves and carry themselves as advisors, mentors, and friends.

Top salespeople are also emotionally involved in their sales relationship. They are concerned that their product or service is the ideal solution to the real needs of the clients. In turn, the customer knows that the consultant cares more about them and their results than they do about the sale.

As a consultant, you are a problem solver, rather than a vendor of goods. When you understand your customer's situation, you know what he or she should or shouldn't buy. This helped me understand how important it is to do your homework prior to meeting with your prospects. Then, you can build on that homework by asking probing questions to understand the customer's needs at a deeper level. You sell by tailoring your product or service in such a way that the prospect concludes that your product is the best solution.

A good comparison I discovered in the book pointed out that consultants are like doctors. Doctors follow three steps: 1) examination, 2) diagnosis, 3) prescription. Sales consultants also follow the same three steps. They must examine the current situation with the prospect, diagnose what the real problem is and then offer a solution or prescription to help them in their lives or business. The essence of your offer should be about how you are going to help the client make or save money.

The next thing I learned is that top salespeople are strategists. They see their goals and then go after them. They are in it for the long haul. They don't worry about every short-term setback and have a blueprint for getting there. They have written time frames to get them to where they want to go. The more clear you are on achieving clear, written goals, the more happy you will be with yourself and your career.

Results are what matter. Tops salespeople are results oriented. They want to help their clients get results; they make the sale by helping the client get what they want. They do the job properly and on schedule. This, I feel, is an incredibly profound thought in my life. If you cannot see results in your work, then what is the point of doing in? If you are going to struggle anyways –shouldn't you at least get the results you want from it anyways?

The next thing I discovered was that the top salespeople usually have two qualities: empathy and ambition. They are sensitive to the client's needs and are focused on both the customer and the sale. Great salespeople are naturally ambitious and I learned that having and that if you show empathy *first*, then you will make the sale later.

The only way you can be a good salesperson is to have your clients like and trust you. A good salesperson is caring, and only truly honest people can really care about their clients if they value themselves enough to reach out.

I've decided to discipline myself to spend more time with prospects and customers who will represent the greatest potential return on time invested. I want to be the best in my field. I know that making a do or die decision to become the best happens *before* someone *actually* becomes the best.

When you effective at what you do, you know what you are doing with every moment of your day and why. You plan and think about your day before you actually do it.

Another great idea I got from this book is that there is no magic bullet or secret that will make you jump light years ahead. There is no substitute for hard, smart work. Unsuccessful people have a short perspective on time and go for the easy way out, sacrificing what's good now for what seems easy. Successful people dedicate themselves for years and years to what they do. They know that "If it's going to be, then it's up to me!"

Successful people know that where they are is a full result of what they have done, and not of "luck." There is no luck. There is only skill, and the law of cause and effect. Truly. If something happens, it is because something made it that way. It is not a matter of "being in the right place, at the right time." What happens to you in your life is entirely dependent on you, and the results that you get from that. Successful people know this, and use it as a guiding principle against everything they do. People who are unsuccessful hope that it doesn't matter.

What you sow is what you will reap. If you put hard work, self-discipline, willpower, and persistence into something, then you will get out respect, status, esteem, sales success, and financial achievement. If you are not happy with something that you are reaping, then it is your responsibility to change it.

Just as a farmer has to plant different crops to get different plants, you have to plant different thoughts and activities if you want to reap different results.

This book is chock full of great insights, and I'm not even a quarter through the notes I took on this book. However, I know that the principles and lessons I've learned from it will prove invaluable to my business.

Book 4:
Business Brilliant by Lewis Schiff

The book *Business Brilliant* is fascinating because it takes seven common beliefs or ideas and our society and shows how the wealthy and the middle class think differently about these ideas.

In fact, the author based his research on interviews with some of the most successful business leaders today. In his introduction, he says:

"…This book seeks to identify what makes certain people brilliant in the business field, what it takes to be 'Business Brilliant.' In the coming pages, you will see how Business Brilliance…has little to do with IQ or education….But most important, the seven Brilliant Business principles in the coming chapters will help you learn about yourself. You'll see why it is just as important to follow the money as it is to follow your passion. Why a 'big idea' won't help you succeed, but the person in the cubicle next to you probably can. Why your network for people needs fewer people, not more. And why you're better off doing only the few things that you do exceptionally well. You'll also learn about some behaviors that might be holding you back. Why you fail to ask for what you want at the moments you're most likely to get it. Why you feel bad when you win a negotiation. And why failure itself is a bad thing only if, like most people, you try to push it out of your mind by taking on something new."—pp. 4-5.

He continues:

"I didn't figure out these principles on my own. They are the products of years of original research, careful study, persistence through setbacks, and lots of help from other people. In fact, the book you are holding is the product of all seven of the Business Brilliant principles it explores."

" In the past six years, household net worth in the United States has fallen by trillions of dollars. The Census Bureau estimates that Americans lost more than one-third of their net worth between 2005 and 2010. White-collar unemployment, meanwhile, has lingered around 6 percent, a number not seen since the 1983 recession, 30 years ago....Even before the 2008 world economic crisis, it was already clear that the old rules of the baby boom generation were dying and would no longer apply in a new world of global communication and competition." –pp. 14-18.

He concludes with this thought:

"What is it that you 'know' right now about money that just might not be true? What do you know about yourself, and your ability to sample a few new ideas?" –p. 19.

This book can relate back to those principles that I've learned in other books, that you need to analyze the talents you have honestly. Take what you have now, and start moving in a direction. He then goes on to talk about why most small business fail, and why

1. Do what you love, but follow the money.

Schiff says:

"More than 7 in 10 middle-class survey respondents said 'doing what I love and allowing the money to follow' was important to their financial success. [However], just 2 in 10 of our self-made millionaire survey respondents agreed with that statement."

This shows that the mindset difference between those who have money, and those who do not. People with money follow what they love *and* the money, but the middle class de

This is why most small business models will fail. Because they believe that they can just build it, and people and money will just flow in. What they don't realize that money follows principles of attraction, and doesn't flow to those whose products are "good" or "bad." I'll talk about that more in Dan Kennedy's *Wealth Attraction*. But for now, realize that money only goes where there is interest in something. The reason that the Rich differentiate from the middle class is that they are not afraid of going out, finding people who might want what they have, and giving it to them for a price. This is why the rich stay rich, and why the poor get poorer. He continues;

"Why don't more middle class people do what they love and follow the money? Why does one-third of the middle class acknowledge the value of having equity in one's work while doing nothing to pursue it?"

Because some people fear money, don't want to ask for money, or don't know how to handle it, they assume that it will flow in whenever it needs to be there. This is false. If you build it, people will not necessarily come. You have to create ways for people to find it, or it will never get out there. This is a good constructive model for me, because now I know that money is not random, or even scary. Money follows rules, just like everything else.

2. Save less, earn more.

Schiff explains:

"In the Business Brilliant survey, about 7 in 10 middle-class respondents agreed that 'cutting back expenditures to help accumulate wealth' is important to their financial success. About the same number cited 'cutting back on little luxuries' as being important. The 2008 financial crisis failed to shake middle-class confidence in these ideas, despite the devastating toll exacted on many retirement accounts. In fact, the surveys conducted before and after the crisis showed almost identical levels of support for the idea that you can save your way to riches.

"Self made millionaires, though, take the extreme opposite view. Only about 1 in 10 say that cutting back on little luxuries or reducing expenses has anything to do with accumulating wealth. To self-made millionaires, financial success is achieved by increasing what comes in, not restricting what goes out. Savings are a fine thing, but those who have gotten wealthy didn't get there by saving. Savings and investments only preserve what you've gained by other means, by working and following the money." –p. 49.

This principle really speaks for itself here. You can really only become rich by increasing flow into your account. The money never could have gotten the money there in the first place if you didn't attract it.

The most interesting section of this chapter talks about the difference in asking between men and women when people acquiring jobs. The principle applies to asking for the sale as well. According to studies, "more than half of the male graduates had asked for more money (57 percent) but only 7 percent of the female students had. Instead, 93 percent of the women (and about 4 out of 10 of the men) had accepted their initial salary offers with no questions asked, even though they'd been specifically advised to ask for more. The survey also revealed that there was a significant reward for asking. Average pay for students who negotiated—men and women alike—was $4,305 higher, a 7.4 percent premium above salaries of nonnegotiators. Almost all the pay disparity between men and women could be attributed to the fact that the men were eight times more likely than the women to ask for the money." –p. 52.

Lewis Schiff says:

"[Fear] is the number one factor preventing people from earning more money....Survey results show why earning more money is all about managing your natural unease with fear and personal rejection. Those unafraid to ask for more, like self-made millionaires, will always earn more than those who fear rejection." –pp. 60, 62.

Why don't we ask a little more in our lives? It makes a big difference. People who asked more are the people who are pioneers, who made it to the moon, who stormed beaches. You will be surprised what you will get out of your life if you just ask a little more.

3. Imitate, don't innovate.

Author Lewis Schiff says that "7 out of the 10 of the middle-class survey respondents said that they believe it takes a 'big or new idea' to become wealthy. Only 3 out of 10 self-made millionaires agreed."

The book details the story of Gary Kildall and Bill Gates and how Gates imitated the operated system that Kildall created and then bought an operating system from Seattle Computer Products (SCP) called QDOS (for Quick and Dirty Operating System) and modified it to create its MS-DOS (Microsoft Disk Operating System). Kildall had created the original idea, but was slow in delivering what IBM wanted in order to create new computers. Gates was much more committed to the business process of following the money instead of innovating. He imitated what had already been created and released it on time for IBM even though there were many bugs in the software. Kildall finally perfected his product, but he was too late to the party. By then, IBM had moved on with Microsoft's product and Kildall's company disappeared into oblivion.

This gets to a important business lesson. I've learned that acting on normal ideas, is much better than waiting on great ideas. People who take action are rewarded. Dan Kennedy's *Wealth Attraction* has the same general idea. History is full of individuals who came up with an original idea or invention, but who didn't profit from it over a long period of time because they were more focused on the innovation than the business application it would have for them.

Schiff says:

"Behind the development of any major invention you'd care to name—the telephone, the light bulb, the automobile, the television—there are legions of broken and disheartened men like Gary Kildall who might be considered the true inventors. Thomas Edison did not invent the light bulb. Joseph Swan had held the British patent for 18 years before Edison introduced his 'improved electric lamp' in 1878. And Henry Ford did not invent the automobile. George Selden of Rochester, New York, patented the 'safe, simple and cheap road-locomotive' in 1895, while Ford was still laboring as a mid-level engineer in Edison's electric company."

"The names Swan, Selden, and Kildall are now largely forgotten because the myth of the lone inventor possessed by a brilliant idea is a powerful one in our culture. 'We like to hear a good story about someone who's ingenious and comes up with a great idea and sees it through,' says Stanislav Dobrev, a University of Utah professor who has studied the history of innovation. '[But] that's not true most of the time.' Dobrev researched the 2,197 car company start-ups in the United States between 1885 and 1981. The first 25 leading car companies were all defunct within 15 years, contributing to Dobrev's conclusion that it pays to be a latecomer, an imitator." –pp. 73-74.

Schiff continues:

"A survey of a far more elite group of business owners reveals the same general aversion to innovation. In 2005, Amar V. Bhide of the Harvard Business School interviewed 100 company founders from among *Inc.* magazine's 500 fastest-growing private firms in the United States. Only 6 percent of these company founders told Bhide that they started their business with unique products or services. Just 12 percent attributed their success to 'an unusual or extraordinary idea.' Instead, 88 percent cited 'the exceptional execution of an ordinary idea' as the source of their high growth and success."

"There are strong echoes of these results in the Business Brilliant survey. Only 3 out of 10 self-made millionaires agree that 'having a big or new idea is a critical factor to becoming wealthy.' Nearly 9 out of 10 said 'it is more important to do something well than to do something new,' which almost exactly mirrored Bhide's findings about 'the exceptional execution of an ordinary idea' among *Inc.* 500

founders."

In the book, the author states that many people want to believe the idea that innovation is what makes everything work. Yet, numerous examples show that acting on an idea is much more important than the idea itself.

There's great story in the book entitled "The Egg of Columbus." As Schiff says: "A legend called 'The Egg of Columbus' illustrates how simple ideas like the Five-Dollar Footlong or the 24-hour copy shop are commonly undervalued because they seem so ordinary and obvious in retrospect. When Christopher Columbus first sailed, most educated people already knew the Earth was round and accepted that the Far East could be reached by sailing westward. So when Columbus returned from his first voyage, not everyone was impressed. Over a late-night dinner with some Spanish gentlemen, Columbus was confronted by the question of whether he'd done anything special, or if he had been the first to follow through on an ordinary idea. Columbus responded by handing the men a hard-boiled egg and asking each of them to attempt to stand the egg on its end. One by one, they tried and failed. When the egg was returned to Columbus, he tapped it gently on the tabletop, cracking and flattening the shell just enough to allow the egg to stand up. 'What is easier than to do this which you said was impossible?' Columbus asked his dinner mates. 'It is the simplest thing in the world. Anybody can do it—*after he has been shown how.*'"

Schiff concludes:

"Damien Hirst (a conceptual artist who is the richest artist in the world) often hears people react to his work by telling him that anyone could do what he does. In 1995, he told the *New York Times*, 'It's very easy to say, 'I could have done that.' After someone's done it. But I did it. You didn't. It didn't exist until I did it. It's like me saying I could have written 'She Loves You.'"

"In similar ways, the Five-Dollar Footlong (which increased sales at Subway in 2008 – it's first year by 17 percent while revenues sagged everywhere else in the fast food industry) and the 24-hour copy center (begun by Kinko's imitating the all night convenience store) might seem in retrospect like the natural, obvious business tactics that any company in a similar situation might have made. But that interpretation is no different than the criticism Columbus faced. It overlooks the persuasive efforts, the commitment, and creative problem solving it takes to deliver on any idea, even an ordinary one….Just as society so often exalts innovation, it often denigrates or dismisses the significant challenges posed by executing on ordinary ideas. And since ordinary ideas are, by definition, much more common than *extra*ordinary ideas, executing on them has a far greater impact on most companies' profits." –pp. 83-84.

The key lesson I learned here is that implementation of a great idea from someone else that is already working is better than a new idea.

4. Know-how is good, 'know-who' is better.

Schiff says that in his *Business Brilliant* survey that "nearly 9 in 10 middle-class survey respondents believe that financial success requires putting one's own capital at risk. Less than 4 in 10 self-made millionaires believe in the need to risk any of one's own capital."

The book details Warren Buffet's strategy of how he built his company with other people's money after failing with his own personal investment in a Sinclair gas station in the early 1950s. The first principle we talked about today was following the money. If you were to have a second principle, it is to follow those who have money. Buffet's strategy was to set up his business so that he always came out on the winning side of the equation. If you study Buffet's life and his business strategies, you'll see that he was quite aggressive about how he went about making his money in the beginning of his life. But, the important lesson is that he learned how to make money without risking any of his own capital (like he had in his first failed business venture). He had the philosophy "heads I win, tails I don't lose."

The book talks a lot about Guy Laliberté's success with Cirque du

Soleil. His success came from his connections with government leaders in Quebec and private donors who helped his business keep going when he really struggled in the beginning. Schiff recounts in *Business Brilliant* that Guy Laliberté was a 'master networker. He gave circus tickets to everyone he thought he could use for future purposes. He treated them like kings. He knew that it would be well worth it down the line, and he turned out to be right.' Laliberté did these things because he had to. He had no other way to keep his pet project and his sole source of income alive. In that sense, he and Hirst encountered similar problems and came up with similar know-who solutions....Both Laliberté and Hirst figured out at an early age that achieving their career goals required them to follow the money, which in turn required them to follow people with money.... Laliberté needed years of generous backing from public and private funders because Cirque shows were expensive to produce. They were more Broadway than Barnum and Bailey, and that was a big part of what made Cirque so special. Laliberté never could have worked his way up from fire-breathing street performer to $1 billion in annual ticket sales without his know-who, without other people and their money" –pp. 101-103.

Schiff concludes with this observation:

"About 750,000 new small businesses open up in the United States every year, and another 750,000 small businesses shut down. About 90 percent of the closed businesses report no losses to creditors because the companies were in debt only to their founders. Like most small businesses, they were run by sole proprietors who relied only on their credit cards and other personal resources for cash reserves and capital. The irony is that many of these small businesses fail because the sole proprietors run out of funds just as they reach the brink of success. This may sound counterintuitive, but when a business begins to grow, expenditures almost always climb more quickly than revenues. Fast growth, which should be a good thing, often causes undercapitalized companies to overextend themselves, make clumsy mistakes, and fail. This is why so many small business owners become slaves to their creations. They are overworked, underpaid, in debt, and teetering at the edge of insolvency—and this is especially true of those whose businesses are succeeding and growing." –p. 103.

Schiff also says about this principle:

"Networking of this kind isn't easy. It goes against certain natural instincts that dictate how 'birds of a feather flock together.' What's more, studies reliably show that the vast majority of people are uncomfortable in situations that necessitate their being the least-affluent member of any group. One famous experiment, repeated many times, shows that most people say they would feel happier earning $33,0000 in a workplace where everyone else makes $30,000 than if they were earning $35,000 in a workplace where everyone else makes $38,000. They would be happy to sacrifice $2,000 a year in salary just to enjoy being top dog in a lower-paying workplace. For most people, it's not enjoyable to be at the bottom of the pecking order, even if the reward is greater net income."—p. 111.

I thought this was really interesting. It is important to overcome feelings of inferiority to ask for and get more out of life.

One final thought by Schiff which I think is extremely insightful:

"The network effect suggests that this is how you can make your own luck. Self-made millionaires like luck. They believe in it. The Business Brilliant survey show that 8 out of 10 consider luck as important to their financial success. In fact, they value luck far more highly than 'getting a good formal education,' which only 3 out of 10 consider important. Among the middle class, however, the ratio is reversed. About 6 in 10 believe education is important while just 4 in 10 say the same about luck. The middle class tends to favor know-how over know-who, which seems unfortunate. The research shows, and the experience of our self-made millionaires seems to back it up, that if you don't tend your network, if you don't seed it so your opportunities are magnified, then when it comes to becoming Business Brilliant, you are literally out of luck." –pp. 113-114.

This principle made me want to work harder at associating with individuals who can help me get to where I want to go. This has been true in my life, that whoever I choose to associate with is who I become. If you want to be successful, stick around people who are going where you want to be going, or are at where you want to be.

5. Win-win is a loser.

This portion of the book talks a lot about the importance of negotiating and asking for what you want but doing it in a way that benefits you. The biggest idea is that of the 'least-interest principle' which is that "in any relationship, especially a business relationship, the person with the least interest in continuing the relationship is the one with the greatest power for setting its terms. The weaker your interest, the stronger your leverage....[In other words], being ready to walk away from a deal is your best guarantee that the deal will work for you." –p. 118.

The book details how former SNL head writer Adam McKay worked out a two year contract with SNL producer Lorne Michaels when he wanted to leave for film projects. Because he was willing to leave, he was able to negotiate out an experience that helped him launch his film career as a feature film director. Today, he is one of comedy's top 5 comedy directors who has consistently worked with Will Ferrell (with whom he developed a relationship at SNL).

The lesson Schiff details in the book is that as individuals become more and more wealthy, they are able to structure deals in ways that are most beneficial for them.

In other words, because they don't need the deal to survive, they are able to negotiate terms that are much more advantageous for them.

Shiff quotes Bill Gates who once said: "You don't get what you deserve in business. You get what you negotiate." Schiff says that there are three principles for successful negotiation—stick to high goals, understand the opposing party's perspective, and set a point at which to walk." This section helped me realize how important it is to negotiate in a way that helps you get what you want in business.

6. Spread the work, spread the wealth.

Schiff says from the Business Brilliant study that "nearly 9 out of 10 self-made millionaires said that when it comes to tasks they are exceptionally good at, they are very likely to delegate those tasks to people who do them better. By contrast, 2 out of 3 middle-class respondents said that when faced with such tasks, they would likely 'do those tasks anyway.'"

Two fascinating examples shared in the book detail entrepreneur Jay Thiessens who announced in 1998 that even though he was running a $5 million dollar a year company, he didn't know how to read. He would postpone business decisions during the day and take everything home to his wife to read to him and then he would delegate decisions out to others on his staff.

Richard Branson, who is dyslexic, today is worth $4.2 billion thanks to the hundreds of products and services bearing the Virgin brand name. Branson "freely admits that he's not good at the details. He is now in his sixties and hasn't held day-to-day responsibilities in any business since he was a teenager. He's never even learned how to read a financial spreadsheet. Once, at a board meeting, Sir Richard kept mixing up the terms 'net revenue' and 'gross revenue' until a staff member took him aside and drew a picture of a net catching fish to illustrate the difference for him. Branson is able to run the business this way because each of the "200 or so product lines is a separate stand-alone corporation, controlled by Virgin but run by a team of entrepreneurs who hold significant equity stakes. Branson has explained that he never wanted Virgin to have 'a vast head office and a pyramid of command from a central board of directors. I am not saying that such a structure is wrong...It is just that my mind doesn't work like that." He once said: "If I could read a balance sheet...I wouldn't have done anything in life."

Schiff says:

"If a reading disability, or any disability, might be considered a gift, it's because some disabled people learn to accept their personal limitations at a young age. They give up trying to fix their weak points and instead they seek opportunities to show what they do best. By the time he was twenty-two, Paul Orfalea (founder of Kinko's) had already accepted that he would have to start a business of his own because he knew he was a miserably inept employee. Charles Schwab has noted, 'I've been able, I think, to recognize my strengths and my deficits...I think that probably has been the single most important benefit I received from having this learning issue early on in my life."

Choosing to delegate what you are not good at is a strength that the most successful business owners all adopt early in their careers. "Fewer than 1 in 10 self-made millionaires said they were interested in attempting the unfamiliar. If they're not exceptionally good at something already, the millionaires would rather not start learning now." This is a big difference between how the middle-class and the wealthy think. The wealthy understand the value of their time and delegate as much as they can to others who can do the job just as well or better than them.

Schiff makes this important distinction:

"Each day, middle-class employees dutifully take up certain tasks that require them to engage their weaknesses. They feel conscientious about working with their weaknesses, and hope that the practice will shield them from future reproach and failure. Meanwhile, self-made millionaires are spending each day avoiding their weaknesses in order to stay focused on their strengths—where distinction, fulfillment and profits are found. Hour by hour, day by day, the middle-class people protect themselves by becoming more well-rounded and ordinary, while the millionaires enrich themselves by becoming more specialized and extraordinary." –p. 150.

This section helped me realize that I need to learn to delegate as my business grows.

7. Nothing succeeds like failure.

Schiff says: "About 7 in 10 self-made millionaires said that 'setbacks and failures have taught me what I'm good at. Fewer than 2 out of 10 in the middle class agreed."

A great example of this is David Neeleman who is the founder of the airline JetBlue. According to Schiff:

"Neelman is a living example of how a mindful response to failure can reap enormous rewards and personal growth. Through soaring victories and terrible defeats, we can see how each of his triumphs was shaped in large part by the lessons he learned and the meaning he derived from all his previous flameouts. Way back in 1983, Neeleman was living in Salt Lake City and running a travel agency that specialized in air-and-hotel packages to Hawaii. A recent college dropout, he had 20 employees, no debt and $8 million in annual revenues when, in December of that year, Hawaii Express airline suddenly went bankrupt. Neeleman's agency relied on Hawaii Express flights for nearly all its travel packages, so when the airline stopped flying and the Hawaiian hotels refused to return Neeleman's advance payments, his travel company ran out of cash and folded.

"Feeling discouraged is a natural response to failure and Neeleman was no different from most people. He was so demoralized by the sudden loss of his company that he considered moving to Arizona and joining his in-laws in the drapery business. But the head of Morris Travel, Utah's largest travel agency, took Neeleman in and gave him a chance to redeem himself. Neeleman soon realized tha the only real mistake he made with his failed agency was that he had to run it with too little capital. When Hawaii Express collapsed, Neeleman didn't have enough cash reserves to ride out the storm. That was a mistake he never made again. From 1984 to 1993, Neeleman helped build Morris Travel into a full fledged airline called Morris Air. He was running 23 jets serving the western states, when his chief concern about the growing carrier was the thinning cash reserves. He persuaded the Morris family to put more money into the company and then he courted investors and raised an extra $14 million, which the airline ended up never touching.

Times were tough in the airline industry in 1993. But Morris Air was one of only two U.S. carriers to turn a profit that year and Southwest Airlines responded by offering to buy the airline for $129 million." – pp. 178-179.

Unfortunately, Neeleman was fired from Southwest five months after he started. He dabbled in venture capital for five years while he waited out a non-compete and started two businesses within the airline industry that helped revolutionalized automated airline ticketing online so airlines wouldn't have to send you a ticket or boarding pass. He also worked with an airline carrier in Canada that didn't affect his non-compete. Then, later he started JetBlue and was overcapitalized when he started which has allowed the airline to be successful right out of the gates. Most successful individuals in business had devastating failures in the beginning. If you study the lives of entrepreneurs W. H. Macy, Henry J. Heinz and Colonel Harland Sanders you can see examples of their legendary determination to overcome adversity.

Schiff makes this statement about the importance of failure in success. He says:

"Discussions about failure are almost always more productive than discussions about success. Don't take my word for it. Amy Edmondson, Harvard's resident expert on failure, puts it this way: 'When facing an uncertain path forward, trying something that fails, then figure out what works instead is the very essence of good performance. Great performance, however, is trying something that fails, then figure out what works, and telling your colleagues about it—about both the success and the failure.' The result, Edmondson says, is what she calls 'execution as learning.' Discussing failure along the way is how to get work done while also considering how to do it better." –pp. 178-186.

The last part of the book explains the importance of mastering the mundane processes in your business. He explains four things you can do to make a LEAP in your business:

Learn – spend more time and effort discovering what you do best

Earn – maximize the profits for everything you do

Assist – cultivate networks of friends, associates and partners who can help you get to the next step

Persist – see setbacks as an important and necessary part of your success

In summary, the seven principles I learned about in this book are:

1. Do what you love, but follow the money.
2. Save less, earn more.
3. Imitate, don't innovate.
4. Know-how is good, 'know-who' is better.
5. Win-win is a loser.
6. Spread the work, spread the wealth.
7. Nothing succeeds like failure.

I know that if I follow these principles in my business, it will help me to have the mindset that I need to succeed.

Book 5:
EntreLeadership by Dave Ramsey

I liked this book because it talks a lot about developing your leadership skills and becoming a leader who is pulling, and helping the team to victory, not pushing employees around. It talks about the difference between a leader, someone who shows people what to do, and someone who was in the position a little longer, and who bosses people around. The book taught me a lot about employee's versus team members (which will be helpful when I grow Phase II of my business).

The entire focus of the book is to help entrepreneurs to become great leaders so they can hire great team members to help them build their businesses.

One thing I found really interesting in this book was his advice on dealing with employees who don't follow the rules. He said:

"[A reprimand] might be as simple as sitting down and reminding someone that our office opens at eight thirty and if they come in at eight forty five they are a thief. I am paying them and when they are late they are stealing. Ouch. That makes the point, and it's true. Some people view tardiness as a harmless behavior but when we put it in those terms—that it's stealing—it helps them see how seriously we view it.

He continues:
"A reprimand done properly should do five things:
1. *Be short.* Don't camp out and spend an hour verbally assaulting someone.
2. *Be uncomfortable for everyone.* If you love reprimanding people you are a bully. You should not avoid, but neither should you relish, giving a reprimand.
3. *Attack the problem.* Love the sinner and hate the sin. Ken Blanchard, in his classic *The One Minute Manager*, says to use the 'Reprimand Sandwich' when you are doing a reprimand. Praise the person and their good qualities, hit the problem behavior directly and hard, then remind the person of their value to you personally and to the organization. Praise, problem, then praise again makes a nice sandwich. I have been guilty of serving a reprimand sandwich with no break, and from personal experience I know it didn't have the long-term desired effect.
4. *Be private.* Never reprimand someone in front of someone else; you will lose their loyalty forever.

5. *Be gentle.* You are teaching and course-correcting in a reprimand, so you owe it to the person to be brutally clear, but you can do that with kindness." –*EntreLeadership*, p. 156.

He also has shown that theme of "What he does matters" throughout the book. This has been an excellent book, and I am sure that it will help me as I grow my company into success.

Book 6:
No B.S. Wealth Attraction by Dan Kennedy

There are three main principles I learned from this book. The first is to be somebody. Secondly, to be somewhere, and finally, to do something.

The first principle is to be somebody. This section talks a lot about becoming a celebrity and becoming an expert in your field. You can elevate your status by writing books, publishing newsletters, putting on events, and learning to use the media effectively to feature yourself in everything you do. In other words, you've got to build your own brand.

By building your own brand you not only make yourself more interesting from a marketing standpoint, you add value for your customers and clients. You should always seek opportunities to take pictures with celebrities. Here is a picture my Dad and I took with Hall of Fame NFL Running Back and Dancing with the Stars Champion Emmitt Smith about a year ago at a business conference we attended:

The next principle this book taught is about creating expert status. Expert status is self-created and self-manufactured. You can make yourself a world-class expert in something by studying every available resource an hour a day for just one year. This is important because if you know more than any other person in your target audience, you automatically become an expert. No one cares at the end of the day whether you are a certified expert or a self-made expert. What they want is results. When you are perceived as an expert, you can charge 5 to 20 times more than the market norm. It also lets you pick which clients you want to work with.

Next, I learned about the principle of being somewhere. Wealth won't find you if you are at home slouched on or hiding under the couch. In other words, you need to put yourself where opportunity can occur. Enormous wealth and fame come from relocation, not in the geographic sense, but in terms of media or market space. It is important to be everywhere that's relevant, everywhere your ideal customers or clients are, and be omnipresent in these environments. Most people are comfortable in only a few places in their lives. Most prefer to stay in a comfort zone. In order to be successful, you must be in more categories or places than any of your competitors, and thus, you must move out of your comfort zone to get the results you need. This part of the book made me ask myself: Where are my best clients going to be? How can I get in touch with them? What do they read, watch, and listen to? Where do they go and congregate?

For my business to be successful, I must pay attention to these questions. You'll see in Part II of this book, how I've answered them as I've put together my business plan.

I really liked this quote in the book by Texas Bix Bender who said: "Just because you're following a well marked trail, don't mean that whoever made it knew where they were going." You've got to understand and know your own path.

The last part of this book I want to talk about is to do something. Gary Halbert said, "Motion beats meditation." It is better to take action and fail than to stay standing still.

The miracle only comes when you work for it. You are the miracle. I especially loved that Dan Kennedy relates about Lee Iacocca blowtorch method. He says:
"Iacocca led Chrysler back from the brink, restoring its profitability, marketplace strength, and even repaying loans guaranteed by the government ahead of schedule. Factory workers caught him walking around and suggested that one of the cars would make a great convertible. He told them to get a blowtorch, cut the roof off, let him drive it around and see how people reacted. And the rest, as they say, is history. The relaunch of the convertible by Chrysler probably attracted more media and public attention and brought more money to Chrysler at a faster pace than any other idea ever acted on in the company's history. All because there was that rare CEO in place who heard a good idea and immediately acted on it. No design committees, no focus groups, no endless meetings of engineers, no long-delayed prototype. *A blowtorch*."—p. 82.

Another great quote I liked was:
"I often say, if poor people knew how shockingly ordinary millionaires were, there'd be a lot more millionaires. One of the biggest erroneous ideas preventing poor people from getting rich is that the rich are somehow smarter or possess some 'magic gene' that separates them from the masses in terms of aptitude or capability. Nothing could be further from the truth. I work very closely, day in and day out, with many millionaire and multi-millionaire entrepreneurs, and I assure you, we aren't that much smarter than the clerk at the corner convenience store. I have clients personally earning millions of dollars a year who forget to put on their shoes when they leave the house, have walked through the screen door on the front of my house without noticing it was there, are woefully dysfunctional managers, incredibly disorganized, slow readers, can't do math, etc. In fact, one, who has built a national chain of tax preparation offices serving

hundreds of thousands of clients can't, himself, add two numbers together without a calculator and couldn't decipher a financial statement if you put a gun against his head. The richest real estate investor I work with was a car mechanic, another a prison guard. But there is one thing they all do that the vast majority of the population doesn't. The 'little' difference is the subject of [Robert] Ringer's book: these people take action."—pp. 83-84.

There is a long list of reasons you can't start now. That list is completely useless. It is best to crumple it up and throw it away. You are ready now. Everyone has one good idea, skill, or talent that they can make money from. There is no wealth to be found in an idea. The wealth is found in acting on ideas.

When you consider the quality of ideas versus the execution of ideas, the execution always wins. A great story I really like in the book talked about a man named Joe Cossman. He is best known as the man who popularized The Ant Farm in the 1950s. Kennedy says:

"Joe was a mail-order marketer who made ten different million dollar fortunes by finding ten different, existent, under-marketed products and bringing them to different avenues of distribution. He invented nothing. And, as he was the first to admit, he didn't do a thing anybody else couldn't do. As an example, he found a product, 'fly cake,' being manufactured and sold to the military, hospitals, and other institutions in bulk to be put into buildings to trap and kill flies. He secured mail-order rights and sold it to homeowners, initially with small magazine and newspaper ads, then through countless catalogs. The manufacturer could have done it, but didn't—didn't experiment with any means of selling the product except the one method he started with."

He continues: "The story of The Ant Farm is even more instructive. When Joe found it, the manufacturer was selling it only to schools, as a teaching aid for biology and earth-sciences classrooms. He recognized that kids would love to have this thing for themselves, and turned it into a blockbuster success as a toy. Joe told me he rarely went a week or two without hearing from a schoolteacher somewhere who said, 'You know, I had the idea to do this before you did.' I'm sure thousands of teachers did. None acted on their idea."—pp. 88.

These were just a few principles that I found valuable in this book. I learned that you must act on a good idea to become successful. If you do not act on an idea, you will never get what you want. It will always be floating just out of reach. If you want an idea to make money, you have to act on it.

Book 7:
The System is the Secret by James Karl Butler (my Dad!)

This book was an interesting read because my Dad wrote it. You don't really know too much about a person until you get inside their head, and learn their thoughts, and it was interesting to see how reading this affected my relationship with my dad. This book covers sixteen systems that businesses need to run properly. An interesting point made by Carrie Wilkerson says it better than I could; "Systems are not sexy, but they really do drive everything we do."

Since I am just starting my business, lead generation seemed to be the most important chapter to write about, and to apply into my business now. There is a simple three-step process that he goes over to generate leads. These steps are:
1) Generate leads
2) Inform and educate about limited time offers
3) Sell products

81% of sales close after the fifth contact. And only 10% of businesses stay dedicated that long to ensure that the sale happens! That surprised me a lot and explained why there aren't more successful salespeople and businesses.

He also talked about the three categories of leads. These are:
1. Hot Leads - Leads ready now would be prospects who have predetermined need and who have requested information from

your web sites (catalog request, special reports, etc.) about a specific product and who have scheduled an appointment or want to talk now about how they can utilize your products or services.

2. Warm Leads – leads at trade shows or leads generated by those who come to your web site and who aren't currently needing your product or service, but will soon

3. Cold (Bad) Leads – leads of those who have just purchased something else who may or may not realize that they *could* buy something from you someday.

This helped me realize that I need to focus more on attracting hot and warm leads to my new business.

On pages 145-153, he lists the twelve categories of lead generation. He says:

"There are twelve main ways to generate leads for your business. I'd like to explore each of them briefly and then give you an assignment to determine how many leads you are generating from each category. In fact, you may realize that you don't even really know where your leads are coming from and which methods are the most effective and productive for you."

These twelve areas are:
1. **Direct Marketing**
Within this category, here are twelve ways this can be done:
1) *Direct mail*
2) *Radio*
3) *Business Card with Offer*
4) *Telephone Invitation / Follow-up*
5) *Movie ads*
6) *Ads in shopper's mailers (local publications mailed into homes).*
7) *Ambassador cards*
8) *Catalog*
9) *Newsletter*

10) *LTOs (Limited Time Offers)*
11) *Upsell in business*
12) *Bounce back coupon*

I really liked this quote in the book by Dan Kennedy: "People read your ad, call your place of business, ask a question, the receptionist answers it, and that's it—no capture of the caller's name, address, email, etc. and no offer to immediately send a free report, gift, coupons. That is criminal waste. It cost money to get that call. Doing nothing with it is exactly the same as flushing money down the toilet. Please go and do so, right now, so you internalize the feeling. Take the largest bill you have in your wallet (or purse)—a $10, a $20, preferably a $100—go to your toilet, tear it into hunks, let them flutter into the toilet, and flush. You probably won't like it. Good. Remember how much you don't like it every time you fail to follow-up (a lot) on a lead or customer....From now on, nothing you do will just be one thing. There will be a planned sequence of things completed. Any contact by you with a prospect or any contact with you by a prospect will trigger a series of follow-up steps."—No. B.S. *Direct Marketing*, pp. 16-17.

This taught me that any client that comes through is of great value to you, whether you realize it or not.

This section helped outline how I can start marketing to get new leads for my business.

2. Print Ads
Within this category, there are five specific ways this can be done:
1) *Industry Specific Magazine Ads*
2) *Billboards*
3) *Local PR with your story (paid)*
4) *Ads in niche publications*
5) *Pre-sale collateral*

From what I know about print ads, they don't seem to be as effective as other methods, but they still do work.

3. Internet (Google, Google Ad Words, any other site other than your web site)

Within this category, there are fifteen main ways this can be done:

1) Personalized emails
2) Email signature invitations
3) Google Places
4) Domain names that fit key word search terms
5) Auto-responder emails
6) RSS Feeds to your articles
7) Blogs
8) Social media
9) Your own podcast
10) E-zine publications
11) Articles submitted to other web sites
12) Webinar
13) Viral marketing with memes
14) Pay per click ads (Facebook, Google Ad Words, etc.)
15) Reciprocal link exchanges

4. Your Web Site

Within this category, there are eight main ways this can be done:

1) Capturing leads from your site
2) Special Reports, chapter from book or eBook which prospects can download and read
3) Videos explaining next step of sequence
4) "Schedule an appointment" button
5) Upcoming Events
6) Countdown Clock for LTOs
7) About Us Story
8) Lead generation site tied to key words that appears as though it is from a third party source

5. Other Media (television, newsletter, local wedding publications, etc.)

Within this category, there are eight main ways this can be done:
1) Television
2) Newsletter
3) Write in local industry publications
4) Local PR with your story (unpaid)
5) On hold phone marketing
6) Guest on local TV show
7) Online TV show
8) Moving billboard (truck)

6. Events

Within this category, there are six main types of events you can conduct to help you generate leads:
1) Planned marketing calendar events
   - Monthly Promotions
   - Events
   - Client customer appreciation events
2) Trade shows
3) Membership Meetings specifically geared to allow existing clients to bring their friends or acquaintances to get to know you and your business
4) Buying leads from trade shows you don't attend
5) On location events (at the prospect's home or business)
6) Product showcase events (demonstrations in high traffic areas where your prospects are or will be)

7. On Site Advertising

Within this category, there are nine main ways you can generate additional sales or leads for additional sales:
1) Indoor signage
2) Outside signage
3) Window displays
4) Posters
5) Published Star/Story profile (Ebook, published magazine, etc.)
6) Letters from happy clients online or in lobby

7) Employee attire
8) Upsell in business
9) Promote book or the articles you've written

8. Community Advertising

There are four main ways you can promote events within your community to generate leads:

1) Local fundraisers
2) Free or paid seminars or speeches to local groups (Chamber of Commerce promotions, other events where your prospects congregate)
3) Community outreach programs
4) Scholarship offers

9. Industry Web Sites

There are seven main ways you can generate leads from industry web sites and Pinterest:

1) Forums
2) Pictures
3) Testimonials
4) Offers / Promotions
5) Contests
6) Ads on other industry web sites
7) Creating memes that can be posted on your Pinterest page to generate interest and leads to your web site

10. Referrals

There are five main ways you can generate new leads through referrals:

1) Referrals from current clients
2) Referrals from employees
3) Referrals from past clients
4) Gift certificates
5) Video testimonials where current or past clients promote you on your web site that are captured at the point of sale

From what I've read about referrals in all the books I've read, the people who are the most successful salespeople work on the continual sale. They keep doing business with the same clients, and get them to tell their friends about it. Have your clients generate leads for you.

11. Vendors and Affiliates

There are three main ways you can utilize vendors and affiliates to generate leads:
1) Cross marketing promotions
2) Networking events
3) Gifts or bonuses to add value to your sale

12. Employees

There are three main ways you can have your employees generate leads every day:
1) Have every employee making a minimum of 2 outbound phone calls/day or scheduling 2 appointments/day
2) Social Networking (promoting LTOs and interacting with others with whom they have with once a week or once a month posts regarding specific promotions or offers-if applicable)
3) Word of mouth buzz (have them write blog posts or share Facebook posts with their friends)

I really liked how each of these strategies were laid out so clearly. It has reminded me that people will only come if they know about a product, and if it has sufficient interest. It is up to me to create the interest that works best for the most prospects.

Overarching principles I've found from each of the books I've read

A love of philosophers and philosophy is something that I have noticed in studying the lives of success people. To get better, you have to know more. They know that knowledge and improvement is the only way to be able to have a good life. They know that knowledge will empower them to be able to achieve their goals.

They respect the success of others. They see how the people they admire get that success, and they copy them until they get what they planned for.

Good salespeople are enthusiastic, and have lots of energy towards a prospect. They are great listeners, who are observant and let the other guy talk, so they can solve their real problem.

They are comfortable with change for the better. They pay careful attention to ways to better themselves, and work on applying that to their business as well as to their personal lives.

They ruthlessly manage their time. Every second, of every day, they have a schedule. They know where they are putting their time resources, and for what reason. If you aren't aware of a schedule, then you have a bad one. They know that every little day doing a simple discipline over time will yield up big results.

You have to be kind to sell: You have to be a good person to make sales happen, and be willing to listen to real needs the client has. You need to be willing to serve the client, and then you lead them into the close.

They are visionaries with plans: They know what they want, when they will get it, how they will get it, and they work out a deadline to get where they want to go.

They are where they are because they want to be. They are not a victim, and know that what they do determines their success, not some nebulous definition.

They know how to work hard, and work is their play. Not only are they committed to excellence, it radiates off of them. They enjoy what they do, and love working everyday for a goal that they have in mind.

They value connections, and good relationships. They have fantastic relationships with like-minded people, to help skyrocket them into where they want to go. They follow the influence of mentors that will show them how to get where they want to go.

They want, they dream, they move.

They have written plans for every aspect of their life, not just one. They have separate plans for health, spirituality, dreams, business, relationships, and they make sure that each area of the life they want is formed with the correct habits to ensure they get there.

They learn from their mistakes, and from the mistakes of others. They create habits to protect them from making those same mistakes again.

They have systems of execution to help them do things in a specific order.

Part ii:
Learning a New Skill

Since my company Mason James Media is designed to help entrepreneurs develop digital solutions for their business, I did some research and discovered that editing podcasts and developing apps would be a good start.

I initially thought I wanted to design web sites to start with, but I decided I needed to learn more skills in this before I could start marketing and selling this service. I created my web site www.MasonJamesMedia.com, which I can use to showcase what I've been learning and to highlight the two products that I'll start marketing and selling.

I decided to start with podcast editing for two reasons. One, it is skill that I could learn quickly, and secondly, there is a big demand as podcasting continues to grow. Most podcasters don't like the amount of time it takes to edit a podcast episode. Since I could learn this skill,

I could start helping entrepreneurs spend time on what is most important (creating) and I could spend time on editing and utilizing this skill. My dad has a podcast (www.SoundLawsofSuccess.com) and he referred me to a web site (www.PodcastersParadise.com) to learn how to edit podcasts.

I spent about six hours watching videos on how to edit podcasts in Adobe Audition. Once I watched the videos, I actually edited one of my father's episodes. It took me several hours to edit my first episode, but he liked how it turned out and he uploaded it. Now, in the first three weeks after I learned this skill, I have edited many podcast episodes and am looking to expand my customer base and edit for others, similar to my lawn mowing business.

There are many aspects to editing. It is time consuming, but that is where my opportunity is. Many podcasters have money, but they don't have as much time as they would like. With my services, now they can continue to create new episodes, and I can edit them and help them have more time to work on what matters. Now, that I've learned this skill, I am writing a book entitled *The Insider's Guide to Editing the Perfect Podcast Episode*, which I'll release as an eBook on Amazon.com as a way to generate new leads for my business.

PART III:
MY BUSINESS PLAN
Mason James Media
Business Plan

Product: Editing Podcasts

Description:
To begin with, I need a project (or series of projects) that I can specialize in. The first that I can do is podcast editing. Because people with podcasts need to do things than edit their podcast, they can turn it over to me. As this area of my business grows, I plan to start learning and creating apps for businesses.

My Purpose
My plan is to provide time to entrepreneurs who have better things to do with their time than to edit podcasts all day. Because I can do this for them, they will pay me money to do a professional job editing podcasts.

How I can get potential clients (Marketing Plan)
I will create a profile on Fiverr.com to gain new clients.

I will also create ad space at the end of clients videos by editing a podcast episode for free, in exchange for a 15 second ad. This will tell others that I edited the podcast, and that I can help anyone who has a desire for editing needs.

I can get my product out there by creating online ads through Fiverr, through my website, through word of mouth, through CraigsList, through a Facebook group, through a public speaking course, through my own podcast, through my own book, and through referrals from existing clients.

Strategies I can use to give me leverage over my competitors

- *Startup underdog-* As this is a newer field, it shouldn't be hard to rise to the top, especially if podcast editing is only a few years old.
- *I can be slightly cheaper, but do a little more.* Not only that, but I will make sure that I am exceptionally friendly with my client base. I will provide excellent service, or your money back!
- *Exponential Growth.* Podcasting is a rapidly expanding field. More than 400,000 podcasts started in the past year. Because this is such a newer field -there will be people coming in every day who have no idea what to do, or who to depend on. Because this is true, it will be easier to build up a client base of people who trust me.
- ***Charge more over time.*** Based on my low cost, high quality position, I will gain clients quickly and will charge more money as I get better and as my schedule becomes full. When I feel like I have too many clients at the time, and they either have to pay more to get my great service, or go find someone else to do it for them. If I do a good job, these clients will likely stay with me as I continue to serve them. Some may leave, but I will reward the people who stay with me with excellent work and efficiency. I will only do this when I am 100% sure that I will not lose over 25% of my client base.

Competitive Analysis

There are several other companies that currently offer podcast editing services. I discovered that there are four main ways in which people charge for this service. These are:

- Monthly (minimum of 4 episodes)
- Hourly
- Per minute of unedited sound file
- Per minute of final edited sound file

Competitive Research of What Others Are Charging:

Here are six examples of pricing options that I found in the marketplace.

1. $700 a Month
   a. 175 per episode (If weekly)
   b. http://smallbusinesspodcasting.com/i-have-a-podcast/
2. $35 an hour
   a. http://www.rocnred.com/rates.html
3. $47 an Hour
   a. http://www.servesense.com/audio_editing/
4. $1.98 per minute
   a. http://www.audiofilesolutions.com/transcription-services/index.html
5. $60 per hour, 2 hour minimum
   a. http://www.collegefundingresource.com/podcastediting/
6. $500 for ten hours
   a. http://www.collegefundingresource.com/podcastediting/

My Prices
I will charge $25 for a finished 30-minute podcast episode. If the original audio file is longer than 50 minutes (for the 30 minute episode), I will add an additional $5.

Additional pricing is as follows:
- $25 for 30 minute finished podcast
- $30 for finished podcast (with original audio file between 50 and 60 minutes)
- $45 for any single episode between 60 and 90 minutes

For that price, I will edit the episode to remove most breathing, some sound errors, background noise (Like AC), and balance the sound.

Now, that I have begun my business and gotten my first client, my goal is to gain enough clients in the next 90 days who are each paying me $100 to $200/month. When I reach this goal for my podcast editing services, I will make at least $1000/month in revenue. I will continue to grow my business from there.

Expenses
$30 a month to Adobe ($10 for Photoshop, $20 for Audition)
$360 Per Year (In Expenses)
$59.95 for AudioTechnica ATR2100 Microphone (http://www.amazon.com/Audio-Technica-ATR2100-USB-Cardioid-Dynamic Microphone/dp/B004QJOZS4/ref=sr_1_1?ie=UTF8&qid=1421786061&sr=8-1&keywords=audio+technica+atr2100)

My Plan to Build My Business

Phase I
I will first develop my podcast editing services, until my name is big enough that many trust me, and I have a good flow of clients coming in.

I will begin with editing podcasts, so that I can learn how to do it more professionally- for multiple clients, for monthly packages. I can start by developing skill on Fiverr, and charging more as I get more skilled.

Begin Learning app design, as it is a popular field right now. I plan to learn from NathanBarry.com and from Lynda.com. I will add these services once I have money coming in more consistently from my podcast editing.

Put website up for professional use. I plan to create my web site by studying programmer Nathan Barry, his site, and his business plan. My web site will allow me to showcase the skills that I have.

Create a business card. I also will create a business card that I can give to those at conferences I attend. My father will also refer me to podcasters he knows in the podcasting community.

Write an eBook entitled *The Ultimate Insider's Guide to Editing the Perfect Podcast.* This small eBook will be used as a business card, and to use for getting my foot in the door based on principles that I have learned over the past 21 days as I've built my podcast editing business, stories about how what I've done, and how it applies to those business principles.

Over the next several months, I have a goal to start my own podcast to attract other podcast hosts so they get to know me and interview me as a lead generation strategy. My idea is to have a podcast based around teen entrepreneurs, and how they are changing the world. I will focus this on how anybody can make a difference, no matter their age. In the podcast, I will share how I created two successful small business models, and how you other teens can too. I will also share basic principles of life and business that I have learned from the books I've read.

Phase II
I will also employ a referral strategy to get referrals from my new clients. I will give a $10 gift card to those who refer someone to me for a single episode and a $25 gift card if they sign up for my monthly podcast editing service. This will encourage my clients to talk about me to their friends who also have podcasts and need my editing services.

When I have too many clients to handle, I will begin to hire on employees accordingly (most likely part time). I will then continue this pattern until the business can self sustain. I will implement systems where I can to automate it, and have the employees help me to run it. I will lead a small team of employees to bring about big yield. (Where it is making enough profit by the employees alone to where I can work on another startup.)

My goal is to make $1000 per month. Here is how I will do that:

Each weekday, I will only do one job (except for Friday where I can do two because it is only a half day at school). I will do these after school or in the evenings.

This means, I will edit eight to nine podcasts episodes per week (with one per day during the week and 2 to 2 on Friday and Saturdays). So, at $25 / edited episode multiplied by 8 episodes, I would earn $200 per week.

If I edit 10 episodes per week (with one per day during the week and 3 on Friday and 3 on Saturdays) at $25 per edited episode, I would earn $250 per week. That will be $1,000/month.

Since I already have acquired one client who has committed to edit a minimum of 8 episodes per month (2/week), I need four to five more clients to reach my goal.

As my business grows, I will edit two episodes every weekday with four episodes edited on Friday, and 6 episodes edited on Saturday. That will mean that I will edit 18 episodes per week and at $25 per edited episode, I will earn $450 per week. That will be $1,800/month.

At this point, I will raise my prices at least $5 per edited episode and begin to hire additional individuals to help me manage the workload. I won't be able to edit more than 18 episodes per week while I am in school so I will need to hire podcast editors to help me earn more than $1,800 per month.

I plan on reaching these goals with the marketing strategies listed above.

Goals

Originally, my goal was to make $100 by the end of the first two weeks. I accomplished this goal and already have one client that is paying me $200 per month (or $2,400 per year).

I also have the goal to reach out to existing podcasters each week to introduce myself and offer my services. I may even set up a webinar at some point to explain my services and invite podcasters to attend so that I can get several clients at one time. At the very minimum, I will meet one professional podcaster per month (and have at least a 5-10 minute phone call with them).

This book summarizes the business books I've learned from and the principles I'm using to continue building my business.

Over the next 90 days, I plan to add at least three new clients per month so that I will have a total of ten clients who are paying me to edit new podcast episodes each week. I will then seek to gain another ten clients over the following ninety days so that within six months, I will be editing eighteen episodes per week.

Outline of Future Marketing / Business Plan

In phase II, I plan to add the following additional products. At this point, I can hire others to edit my podcasts so that I can learn new skills in app design and web design. I will also offer new offerings with podcast editing using more advanced tools in Audition.

What I have to do to get started:
Build Fiverr Account and start lead generation
Get headshots for pictures on Fiverr and other marketing pieces

First, I will set up my Fiverr account. This will allow me to get clients from all over the world. Then, a website promoting my podcast editing, and my celebrity brand. I am working on the design of my web site now. Then, I will expand with more advertising, targeting those podcasters who I can help with my editing services.

Objective
My market is anyone who has a podcast, but doesn't have the time or desire to edit their podcast episodes. I will make it quick and painless for them to be able to get their podcast uploaded, with proper tags, uploaded to iTunes, Stitcher Radio, tagging, removing breathing, umm-and editing background noises out. I will also enhance the existing audio if necessary.

New Product Development
New products
- Apps
- Web Site Development

Advertising opportunities
- I plan to have a booth at Podcast Movement in Dallas, Texas offering my services
- I also have contacted Interview Connections about my podcast editing service. Interview Connections connects guests with podcast hosts. The owners, Jessica Rhodes knows many podcasters and will be a great referral source for my company.

Client rewards program continuity program
- $10 gift card for anyone who refers one single episode editing
- $25 gift card for anyone who refers monthly client (at least four episodes per month)

Operations and Systems (these are the areas that I will develop and expand as I grow my business)
Operating and control systems
Administrative policies, procedures, and controls
> Process for receiving bills, paying referring companies
> Weekly training meetings
> Monthly / weekly management meetings
> Monitor and control of budgets
> Describe security controls for client lists and proprietary information
Documents and paper flow
> Describe flow of information through business and office
Planning chart
> Weekly marketing meetings (Monday mornings – planning events, promotions, etc.)
> Customer service plan
> Developing team

Marketing calendar (implementing promotions, ensuring market dominance by implementation)

Risk analysis and alternative plans of action

What we will do if:

- Sales projections prove wrong
- New competitor moves in takes clients

Established procedures

Product sales

- Invoicing Clients
- Banking / Credit Cards / Process for Deposits (already have Square set up to process client transactions)

Hiring

Training for new hires on how to edit podcasts

Logistics of training

Quiz to ensure understanding of podcast editing

Contact with Clients

Relationship building (how do we continue to build a relationship with the client so he / she wants to return and do even more business with us?)

Sequence

- Marketing Sequence
- Thank You Sequence (thank you card + gift card)
- Newsletter (to be developed to showcase new podcasts that people can listen to that I edit – as a value added service)
- Development of first time incentives (free podcast edit if they allow you to place commercial before and after podcast content)
- Set up Facebook and Twitter Profiles

Development of Clients Inviting Them to Use Other Services

- Direct mailings
  - o Sequences and marketing flow chart to be developed

- Back end marketing where I contact existing clients to find out need for apps or web site designs
- Referral Marketing
  - o   Reminders to get out referral coupons
  - o   Social media strategies to get others to promote my podcast editing
  - o   Obtain testimonial letters and videos from clients which I can place on my web site
  - o   Thank you referral bonuses (gift cards to give out to those who refer me to others)

PART IV:
BUSINESS DOCUMENTS

My father and I had an attorney register our company with the state of Utah after we filed the necessary paperwork. Here are the copies of the documents we put together for our business.

On the pages that follow, you'll see copies of our original documents created as we set up Mason James Media, LLC.

These include the following:
Articles of Organization
Operating Agreement
Minutes from Our First Meeting
Copy of our Federal Tax ID number (employer identification number or EIN)

Articles of Organization
This document formally organized our limited liability company (LLC). We had to pay $70 to file these organizing documents with the state of Utah.

Our articles of organization defined the purpose and address of our business and the members (which included my Dad and I). The purpose listed in the original agreement is: "The purpose of the business is graphic design, web site design, and interactive marketing services." This document is necessary to show that the company has officially been established and is proof that the business is legal and set up. My Dad explained to me that with this document and our EIN (employer identification number), we could set up our checking account.

Then, we set up an operating agreement. Here is a copy of our operating agreement:

OPERATING AGREEMENT

OF

Mason James Media, LLC

THIS OPERATING AGREEMENT is entered into on this **15th** day of **January, 2015**, by the following individuals as members / managers of the above named Company organized under the Utah Revised Uniform Limited Liability Company Act, Utah Code Ann. § 48-3a-et. seq.:

Jim Butler

Mason Butler

WHEREAS, the Members desire that all activities of the Company be according to the terms and conditions of this Operating Agreement and any amendments thereto.

NOW, THEREFORE, the Members hereby agree as follows:

I.
Name, Principal Place of Business, Duration

The name, principal place of business and duration of the Company shall be as described in the original Certificate of Organization filed with the State of Utah and may be amended from time to time as agreed to by the Members.

II.
Purposes and Powers

The Company may engage in all lawful activities in which a limited liability company may be engaged under the Utah Revised Uniform Limited Liability Company Act and any amendments thereto. Members are authorized to use whatever powers are necessary or convenient to carry out such lawful activities.

III.
Tax and Accounting Matters

3.1. The Members intend that the Company be classified as a partnership for Federal and State income tax purposes. This Operating Agreement shall be interpreted so as to be consistent with the Members' intent.

3.2. The accounting year of the Company shall end on December 31st of each year.

3.3. Each member shall receive from the Company in a timely manner all tax information and documentation required by law.

IV.
Capital Contributions and Loans

4.1. The Members have transferred cash and other assets directly to the Company, the value of which is reflected as set forth in Schedule "A" attached hereto. Additional funds are not required in order to preserve initial ownership percentages in the Company.

4.2. The Company may raise additional capital by borrowing from its Members or third parties on terms agreeable to the Members. Equity interests in the Company may be sold as a means to raising needed capital, but only by majority vote of the Members.

4.3. Members are not entitled to a return on capital contributed, except as provided in this Operating Agreement.

4.4. No interest shall accrue or be paid on the balance of a Member's capital account.

V.
Capital Accounts

5.1. Each Member shall have a capital account. The same shall be increased by the following:

    A. money contributed (or deemed contributed) by such Member;

    b.   the fair market value of property other than money contributed (or deemed contributed) by such Member, net of liabilities secured by such property that the Company is considered to assume to take subject to under I.R.C. Subsection 752 which are secured by such property;

    C. the amount of Company liabilities assumed by such Member;

    D. the Member's share of profits of the Company or other amounts allocated to the Member; and

    E. the member's share of Section 704 (c) property; and

the same shall be decreased by the following:

    F. money distributed (or deemed distributed) by the Company to such Member;

    G.   the fair market value of property other than money distributed (or deemed to be distributed) by the company to such member, net of liabilities secured by such property that such Member is considered to assume or take subject to under I.R.C. Subsection 752;

    H. the amount of the Member's individual liabilities assumed by the Company, not including liabilities described in subsection "b" above;

    I. the Member's share of losses of the Company or other losses or deductions allocated to such Member; and

J. the Member's share of any book depreciation or loss attributable to I.R.C. Subsection 704 (c) property.

5.2. In the event any Member having a loan obligation to the Company is in default, the Company shall have as one of its remedies the right to charge the Member's capital account with all or a portion of the loan amount in default. All that is required is written notice to the Member. "Default" shall include financial insolvency of a Member.

VI.
Valuation

6.1. Contributed property (or property deemed contributed) shall be valued according to fair market value as of the date of the contribution.

6.2. Distributed property (or property deemed distributed) shall be valued according to fair market value as of the date of distribution.

VII.
Profits and Losses

Profits and losses shall be allocated according to the percentages set forth on Schedule "An" attached hereto, unless the Members agree otherwise from time to time.

VIII.
Net Cash Flow and Distributions

8.1. The net cash flow of the Company shall be distributed to Members in proportion to the percentages set forth in Schedule "A" attached hereto at such times and in amounts deemed advisable to the Members. However, at the end of each fiscal year, the Company may distribute to its Members all or a portion of the net profit for the year. The purpose of this provision is to enable Members to pay Federal and State taxes on their distributive shares of the Company's income.

8.2. Upon termination of the Company and after all required debts have been paid, each Member shall receive a distribution in proportion to ownership percentage set forth in Schedule "A".

IX.
Management

9.1. Each Member is also a Manager and shall have one vote. Management decisions by the Members shall be by affirmative vote of a majority of the Members, unless otherwise specified herein.

9.2. One or more Members may be chosen by the required majority vote to carry out management decisions. This Member (or Members) is authorized to do all things necessary and reasonable to accomplish those designs set forth in management decisions, and no specific enumeration of powers is required, except that such Member (or Members) is not authorized to do anything contrary to the Company's stated business purpose. The chosen Member (or Members) shall have authority to carry out management decisions to the exclusion of all other Members.

9.3. The initial Members / Managers authorized to carry out management decisions are:

Jim Butler

(Mason Butler is under age at the time of the signing of this agreement.)

9.4. No Member elected to carry out management decisions shall be personally liable to the Company or its Members for any loss or damage to the Company, unless such loss or damage is the result of fraud, gross negligence or willful misconduct as proven by court order or decree.

9.5. The Company shall indemnify any Member elected to carry out management decisions that is made a party to any threatened, pending, or completed action, suit or proceeding, against cost and expenses, including attorneys fees, judgments, fines, and settlement amounts, actually and reasonably incurred in connection with the action, suit or proceeding.

X.
Rights and Obligations of Members

10.1. No Member shall be personally liable for any debt, obligation or loss of the Company beyond the amount of such Member's capital account

10.2. Members shall have the right to access the books and records of the Company upon reasonable request during normal business hours. This right includes the right to copy documents at the Member's expense.

10.3. No Member shall have priority over another Member in regards to distributions, return of capital contributions or in regards to any other right or obligation.

10.4. No Member has the right to require that his or her interest in the Company be redeemed in whole or in part.

10.5. No Member may withdraw from the Company except through the required majority vote by the Members.

XI.
Admission of New Members

No person shall be admitted to the Company as an additional Member except the required majority vote by the Members.

XII.
Transfer of Member's Interest

12.1. A Member may not sell, exchange, assign or otherwise transfer, nor mortgage, pledge or otherwise encumber all or any part of his or her interest in the Company, whether voluntarily or involuntarily, by operation of law, order of any court, contract, gift, will, intestacy, financial insolvency, division of property in the context of a divorce or separation proceeding, or otherwise, except through the required majority vote by the Members.

12.2. Any transferee of a Member's interest in the Company shall have the status of a mere assignee and shall not be entitled to become, nor to exercise, any of the rights of a Member of the Company until full membership rights are granted through Majority vote by the Members.

XIII.
Dissolution and Termination

13.1. The Company shall be dissolved upon the occurrence of any one of the following:

A. when the duration period of the Company expires;

B. upon the affirmative vote of all Members; or

C. upon the death or financial insolvency of any Member, except the remaining Members may choose by majority vote to continue the business of the Company, which vote must take place within ninety (90) days of the event giving rise to dissolution.

13.2. Upon dissolution, the Members shall wind up the affairs of the Company by conducting an orderly disposition of assets and distribution of proceeds with the following priority:

A. First, creditors of the Company other than Members or former Members receiving payments from a buy-out of their interest in the Company;

B. Second, to Members for any debts of the Company to such Members, including Members receiving payments in buy-out of their interest in the Company;

C. Third, to Members in the amount of their capital accounts after allocation of all profits, losses and special allocations.

If the assets of the Company are not sufficient to return to any Member the full amount of his or her investment, such Member shall have no recourse against any other Member.

13.3. No Member shall be entitled to the return of any specific property contributed to the Company.

13.4. When all debts, liabilities and obligations have been paid and discharged or provided for, and all remaining property distributed to the Members, Articles of Dissolution shall be executed and filed with the State of Utah. Upon issuance of a certificate of dissolution by the State of Utah, the Company shall be terminated.

XIV.
Miscellaneous Provisions

14.1. This Operating Agreement may be amended through a majority vote by the Members.

14.2. This Operating Agreement shall be governed by the laws of the State of Utah.

14.3. The headings in this Operating Agreement are inserted for convenience only.

14.4. This Operating Agreement shall be binding upon and inure to the benefit of the parties hereto and, their respective heirs, legal representatives, successors and assigns.

14.5. Through written financial reports or other appropriate measures, the Company shall advise the Members on a regular basis concerning the financial and business condition of the Company.

IN WITNESS WHEREOF, this Operating Agreement has been executed on the above date by the following Members. By their signatures below, said Members affirm that they have read the foregoing Operating Agreement and are familiar with its contents.

_____

Jim Butler

_____

Mason Butler

My Dad and I signed the original agreements. We also divided out the company so that we each own 50% of the entity. When I turn 18, I'll be able to assume full operational control of the business.

Next, we created a meeting of the minutes of our company. Here is a copy of the minutes from our first meeting:

MINUTES OF THE ORGANIZATIONAL MEETING OF

THE MEMBERS OF

Mason James Media, LLC

a Utah Limited Liability Company

The organizational meeting of the Members of **Mason James Media, LLC** was held at --------*address removed from this book (in original document)*---------- on **January 15, 2015** at the hour of **5 p.m.** Present in person or by telephone were: **Jim Butler and Mason Butler**, who are a Members / Managers of the Company and also constitute 100% of the voting rights in the Company.

Jim Butler called the meeting to order. It was discussed that a Certificate of Organization of the Company had been filed with the State of Utah and that business would commence at that time and that the company would adapt and ratify all business of the company that transpired prior to that date. A copy of said Certificate of Organization was ordered to be inserted in the Minutes as part of the records of the meeting when received.

A proposed form of the Operating Agreement for the regulation and management of the affairs of the Company was presented and adopted by all Members.

The undersigned, being all the Members of **Mason James Media, LLC** hereby vote and consent to the adoption of the following resolutions:

Following discussion, on motion duly made and seconded, it was: RESOLVED, that the **Jim Butler & Mason Butler when he reaches the age of majority** be authorized, empowered and directed to open a Company account with any FDIC insured bank and to deposit therein all funds of the Company, all drafts, checks and notes of the Company, payable on said account to be made in the company name signed by one of those respective parties as may be shown as proper signatures on a signatory card to be filed with said bank.

FURTHER RESOLVED, that the Members are hereby authorized to execute such resolutions (including formal bank resolutions), documents and other instruments as may be necessary or advisable in opening or continuing said bank account. A copy of the applicable printed form of Bank Resolution is hereby adopted to supplement these Minutes is ordered appended to the Minutes of this meeting.

A discussion was held regarding the payment of expenses for the operation of the company.

RESOLVED, that the Members hereby authorized to pay or reimburse the payment of all fees and expenses incident to and necessary for the organization of this Company.

A discussion was held regarding the business address of the company.

RESOLVED, that the address of the company shall be -------*removed--* ------------.

It was agreed that any time during the last week of each year would be the appointed time for the annual meeting of the Members and that adequate minutes thereof would be kept and preserved, and copies thereof furnished to each of the members upon request.

This vote and consent is given pursuant to the Certificate of Organization and pursuant to the Utah Revised Uniform Limited Liability Company Act, Utah Code Ann. § 48-3a- et. seq., and is intended to have the effect of a unanimous vote pursuant to motions duly made allowing **Mason James Media, LLC** to undertake the action specified therein.

There being no further business to come before the meeting, the same was adjourned.

DATED this 15th day of January, 2015.

_____

Jim Butler – Member / Manager

_____

Mason Butler – Member / Manager

We each signed the original agreement.

Then, to finish setting up our company and to be able to open a checking account, we needed to get a Federal Tax ID number or employer identification number (EIN). Our attorney helped us get this set up.

Once we had our legal documents created, we set up a checking account. I was amazed at the amount of paperwork involved in setting up a company and then the checking account, but after an hour or so at the bank, our account was set up. I couldn't be added to the checking account as a signer, but will be able to do so when I am eighteen years old. I deposited my first $120 in sales that I had already made and we got printed checks and a debit card for the business (in my Dad's name) so we could get supplies as we need them. It is exciting to be all set up. Once this was set up, I set up our merchant account processing through Square (www.square.com). We ordered a Square reader online so we can process credit cards. We set up the account so that money received through credit cards would be set up into our new business checking account.

Now that the company is all set up, I am ready to continue building Phase I of my business. I can't wait to grow the business to the goals I've set for myself and that I've laid out in this book.

Conclusion

One of the things that I want to leave you with is that you can build your dreams. If I can do it, so can so. It doesn't matter where you are now. Start immediately! Anyone can find relative success. What you want and whatever you can imagine *is* reachable. All you have to do is be willing to take the steps to get it done. I can assure you with experience that there isn't anything better than standing on top of a goal that you set, and ultimately reaching it. (Except for the miracle of childbirth, but I can't say I ever want to experience that.)

Here are a few of the lessons I learned from this experience:

Doing good habits consistently will get you to any dream you have.

If you don't make time for the big dreams you have, they will never happen.

The making of the product is only 5% of the work.

In fact, the marketing can be more important than the making of it. If no one buys it, what's the point of making it?

You only need a plan to get you out of the starting gate. Start now with one thing.

Charge more on your product with time, as your skill increases.

Wealth doesn't flow to where "Good People" are. Money doesn't respect people, it only follows rules of attractions (attraction created by interest). If it did not, we would not have criminals like Dillinger, or Jesse James. It doesn't say: No! You are bad! We won't go into your hands! It goes where there is interest.

If you build it, people won't come. People only know about things that have a market presence, such as a billboard. I know it seems obvious, but it's true. People only come to a product if it's an interesting message in the right place.

Successful people do the small, daily disciplines to get them to where they are. They are consistent, and determined. They are steady. You don't have to be fast to win the race, but you have to be steady.

Compound interest - your dreams will take care of themselves with time -if you do the daily disciplines, it will fall into your hands quicker than you think. You may be impatient at some times, but things will work out in the end, if you keep up those daily disciplines.

How you live your dreams:

1) Dream as big as you can.

2) Block out the big steps to get there

3) Get started now working toward that goal -A plan to get you out of the starting gate

4) Doing those small, daily disciplines to get you where you want to go

5) Planning sessions weekly to make sure you are making progress towards that eventuality

6) Work out the smaller tidbits as you go -Big plan first, alter course as necessary.

7) Have weekly, monthly, yearly, five years, ten year goals in mind.

Thanks for reading this book and sharing my journey as I've built my company over the past 21 days from idea to business. I've learned so much from the books I've read, from the meetings I've had with my Dad, and from gaining my first clients. It is exciting to be on the way to building my dreams.

About the Author:

Mason James Butler is a sophomore at Karl G. Maeser Preparatory Academy. He is the founder of Mason James Media, an Internet production company that specializes in podcast editing. He is a computer science guru, avid tennis player, and a total goofball. He enjoys creative writing, PC gaming, learning Chinese, reading, and watching SpongeBob Square Pants with his family.

You can visit his web site at: www.MasonJamesMedia.com